Bear's Heart

SCENES FROM THE LIFE OF A CHEYENNE
ARTIST OF ONE HUNDRED YEARS AGO
WITH PICTURES BY HIMSELF

TEXT BY BURTON SUPREE, WITH ANN ROSS

Afterword by Jamake Highwater

J. B. Lippincott Company / Philadelphia and New York

For Remy Charlip

U.S. Library of Congress Cataloging in Publication Data
Supree, Burton.   Bear's Heart.
SUMMARY: A biography of Bear's Heart illustrated with his own drawings done while he and seventy-one other Indians were imprisoned in Florida.
    1. Bear's Heart, 1851-1882—Juvenile literature. 2. Cheyenne Indians—Biography—Juvenile literature. 3. Castillo de San Marcos, St. Augustine—Juvenile literature. [1. Bear's Heart, 1851-1882. 2. Cheyenne Indians—Biography. 3. Indians of North America—Biography. 4. Castillo de San Marcos, St. Augustine] I. Ross, Ann, joint author. II. Bear's Heart, 1851-1882. III. Title
E99.C53B427   970'.004'97 [B] [97]   76-48952   ISBN-0-397-31746-8

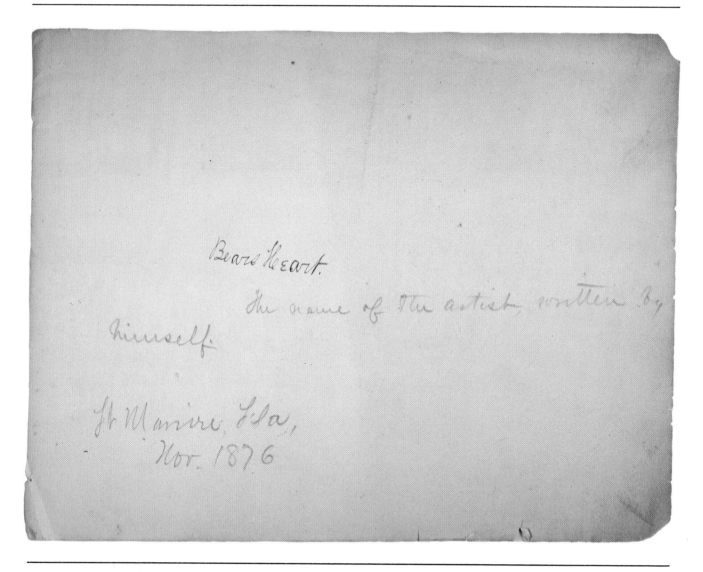

The name of the artist, written by himself

Lieutenant Richard Henry Pratt (standing, left) with Indian prisoners at Fort Marion, Florida, around 1876. Bear's Heart is at left side of the third row. Courtesy Field Artillery and Fort Sill Museum.

Bear's Heart drew these pictures in a school drawing book while he was a prisoner at Fort Marion, St. Augustine, Florida. He arrived at the fort in May 1875 and made this group of drawings in November 1876. The materials he used were colored pencils and inks. The notations on the pictures were written by Lieutenant Richard Henry Pratt.

The book was given to General William Tecumseh Sherman as a gift when he visited the prison on a tour of inspection that November. It now belongs to the Museum of the American Indian—Heye Foundation.

Bear's Heart was born into the Cheyenne tribe in the year 1851. And he grew up in the days when there were still plenty of buffalo roaming the western plains of North America.

This homeland of the Cheyennes was a high, windy country. When the short grass grew richly in the late spring and early summer, the buffalo came together in huge herds. But as the hot weather went on and the grass began to dry up and thin, the herds broke up and scattered to find food.

The Cheyennes trained their horses to run close beside the buffalo so that a rider would have both hands free to use his bow. When the hunt was over, the buffalo were skinned and the meat was brought back to camp. It was the Cheyennes' main food. Some of it was dried in the sun to keep for times when food was scarce. The hides made the coverings of tepees, fur robes for the winter, moccasins, and shields. And the sinews of the buffalo's back and legs made thread for sewing and strings for bows.

The Indians traveled freely over the plains. They packed up their belongings and moved their camps to follow the buffalo and to find sweet water and good grass for their horses.

Cheyennes among the buffalo

As the years passed, settlers moved west along the overland trails. Cattlemen took over rangeland for their herds, prospectors searched for precious metals, towns grew. Railroads divided the land: great crews came to lay the rails, and soldiers came to protect them. Hunters, hired to get fresh meat for the workmen, shot thousands of buffalo. And when the railroads were finished, the noisy trains scared the game away.

Ranchers and farmers had moved into the richest valleys, planting themselves on land the Cheyennes had roamed and loved. And by the time Bear's Heart was a man, the Cheyennes and their friends the Arapahoes had been forced to sign away their land in one treaty after another. They had been pushed, bit by bit, far south and east, from one reservation to the next.

Finally, the Cheyennes wound up on a reservation in western Oklahoma, Indian Territory. But this land was never home to them, and the buffalo were few. Most members of the tribe were unhappy. Chiefs and their bands left the reservation to look for a place where they could live without interference. But there was no such place. And the soldiers pushed them back to the reservation again and again.

On the Canadian River, Indian Territory

Bear's Heart had grown up in the traditional ways of his people. He learned the habits of the animals and the skills of the hunter. The Cheyennes faced many enemies on the plains, and a young man had to prove himself a good warrior as well as a hunter. His life, and the lives of others, depended on his skill. And everyone respected men who were brave, men who led successful raids, even men who took wild, show-off risks and courted danger.

When his father died, Bear's Heart was terribly upset. He unbraided his hair and grieved. One way Plains Indians traditionally expressed mourning was by making an attack on an enemy. When a war party of about twenty young braves left camp to fight Utes, who lived in the mountains of Colorado, Bear's Heart rode off with them.

He grew to be a seasoned warrior. In summers after, he went on many raids, usually to Texas to steal horses. Winter, when the tribe settled into permanent camps, was a bad time for raiding. The dried-out grass the horses pawed up from under the snow didn't give them enough strength and endurance to carry the weight of a rider for such long distances.

Meanwhile, there was no peace or safety for the Indians who stayed on the reservation. The government failed to live up to its treaty obligations. Whiskey peddlers and traders cheated the Indians. Raiders stole many of their horses and went unpunished. Often the Indians were short of food—and the buffalo were far away. White buffalo hunters killed millions of buffalo for their hides and left the meat to rot. The government promised to stop them, but the killing went on all the same.

The Indians were helpless. Those who left the reservation were harassed and driven back; those who stayed found that the government didn't provide for them and couldn't protect them. Everything seemed to get worse, no matter what they did.

Unable to find enough game to provide for their families, and forbidden to prove themselves in battle, the men felt dishonored, useless. In the burning summer of 1874, great numbers of Indians—small bands of young men, large camps of families—fled the reservations, and Bear's Heart was among them. These were not only Cheyennes, but Arapahoes, Kiowas, Comanches. They'd had enough.

Five strong columns of soldiers were sent out to drive the Indians back. The large camps, and even the small groups of Indians roaming the prairies, had a hard time avoiding the troops. They found only a few small buffalo herds, and many of them had to return to the reservations to keep from starving.

The disciplined troops continued the pursuit. Mounted on strong horses, which they fed on grain that they carried with them when the grazing was poor, the soldiers hunted the Indians all through the summer and the terrible winter of 1874 and 1875.

Cavalry, Camp Supply

Some bands, like the one Bear's Heart rode with under war leader Medicine Water, were able to avoid the cavalry. Late in August, when the wild cherries were ripe, they came upon six men out surveying land near Lone Tree, Kansas. To the Cheyennes, surveyors meant more railroads and more settlers and more trouble. They killed all six. And they killed the oxen which hauled the surveyors' wagon and cut off their hindquarters for food.

Now the war party was on the run. They knew they couldn't win in a fight against huge numbers of well-fed soldiers with powerful weapons. But they were angry and frustrated enough to take revenge on any small party of whites they came across.

About two weeks later, Medicine Water led his war party up a ravine behind a hill where John German and his family had camped for the night on their way from Georgia to Colorado. At sunrise, while two of the children were rounding up their cows, Medicine Water's party attacked the wagon and killed German and his wife and three of their children. They took the other four girls as hostages, set fire to the wagon, and rode off, driving some of the cattle. They were hungry and stopped soon to kill the cows and roast some of the meat.

In a misty rain, they started to ride again. They rode for many days. They traveled light so they could move fast, on the lookout for soldiers. They ate once a day, and quickly. If there was no time to go after a buffalo, they killed one of the horses. They traveled all through the nights, talking in whispers, only stopping at daybreak to rest and sleep.

They had difficulty finding the main Cheyenne camps, which had been moved while they were gone, so Medicine Water sent some men to search for them. At last they reached Grey Beard's camp.

When the camp was attacked by the troops two months later, in early November, the two younger girls were freed. And soldiers found the two older girls when another band, led by Stone Calf, surrendered in March.

Bitter weather set in on the icy Texas plains. The big camps were constantly on the move, trying to escape the soldiers. With the buffalo nearly all gone and so little time for hunting, the Indians were starving. Many horses had been lost. Those that were left worked hard and grew weak because it was so cold and the grass so poor. When the troops attacked the camps, the people had to leave their lodges and food supplies, and the soldiers burned them. The miserable Indians began to drift back to the reservations.

In the middle of December, Bear's Heart and two friends, exhausted, left Grey Beard's camp and returned unobtrusively to the reservation. But a few weeks later, Big Moccasin, another Cheyenne, pointed out that Bear's Heart had been with the band that murdered the surveyors and the German family, and Bear's Heart was locked up in the guardhouse.

To wipe out resistance by the Indians, the government decided to punish the hostile chiefs and some of the warriors by sending them to prison in the east. Soldiers lined up the Cheyenne warriors. They picked out four of the chiefs, ten other men, and one woman, Medicine Water's wife, who had been identified—like Bear's Heart—as raiders. Then eighteen more men were picked at random to make a total of thirty-three. The Indians' legs were shackled and they were surrounded with many guards.

Two weeks later, even more soldiers arrived. The Cheyenne prisoners were chained into wagons and taken south that night to Fort Sill.

Bear's Heart and the other Cheyennes only stayed at Fort Sill a little while. Prisoners from other tribes—Kiowa, Comanche, Arapahoe, and one Caddo—were brought there as well.

When it was time for the prisoners to be taken to the nearest railroad, 165 miles east, they were chained into eight army wagons with hay at the bottom. Many Indians had come to see the prisoners start their journey. All during the preparations, the women gathered around the fort and on the hillside and wailed loudly. Families and friends were not permitted to come say goodbye until just before the wagons left.

So the seventy-two Indians began their long trip to exile and prison in Florida. But they all believed that they were being taken away to be killed.

Fort Sill, Indian Territory

Lieutenant Richard Henry Pratt was deeply concerned about what would happen to the prisoners and asked to be put in charge of them. He traveled with them on the grueling month-long journey to Florida.

On the first leg of the trip, they made camp each night with their wagons and tents near fresh running water. The prisoners were in bad shape. They were weak and sick from the many hard months of running and fighting on the prairies with little to eat and no rest or shelter. And they dreaded what was going to happen to them.

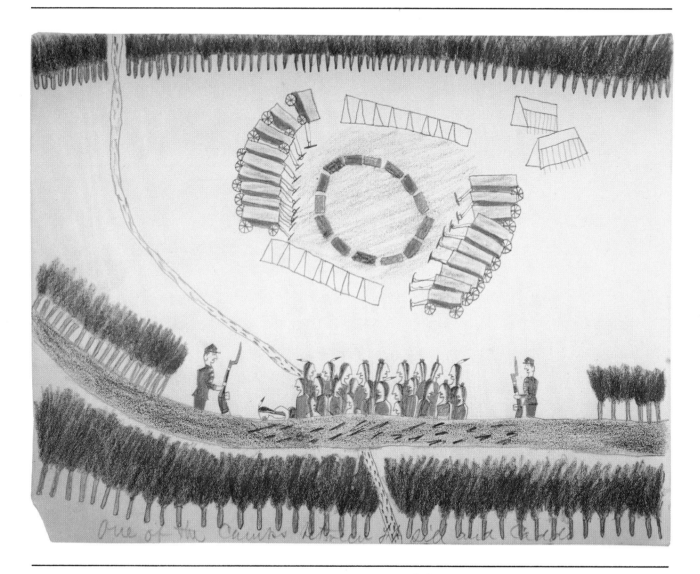

One of the camps between Fort Sill and Caddo

Still in chains, the Indians were taken from the wagons and put on a train. Only one of the prisoners, Lone Wolf, a Kiowa, had ever been on a train before. When the train started, the Indians were curious, but as it began to move faster and faster, some of them were frightened by the speed. They pulled their blankets over their heads and wouldn't look out.

At each of the large stations the train stopped at—St. Louis, Indianapolis, Louisville, Nashville, Atlanta, and Jacksonville—people came to take a look at the prisoners, who were frightened by the inquisitive holiday crowds. Lieutenant Pratt's wife and children joined him on the train at Indianapolis. But Pratt spent most of his time with the prisoners, talking with them through an interpreter in the Comanche language, which many of the Indians understood.

One day, as he went through the train with his oldest daughter, who was six, Pratt stopped to talk with Chief Grey Beard. Grey Beard said that he had only one child, a girl, just about the same age as Pratt's. He asked Pratt, in a voice trembling with sadness, how he would like to have chains on his legs and to be taken far away from his home and his wife and his daughter. But Pratt couldn't answer.

Stevenson, Alabama

Then, late one night, near the state line between Georgia and Florida, the guards woke Lieutenant Pratt to tell him that one of the Indians had jumped out of the window. Grey Beard was gone.

The train slowly backed up. The night was not very dark, and soon Grey Beard's blanket was spotted. The train stopped, and Pratt, the guards, the trainmen, and the passengers began to search through the brush.

After a long while, the engineers said that the train had to start up again or it would not be able to reach the next water tank. Pratt left four soldiers to continue the search, and the train pulled away. But as it started to move, Grey Beard jumped out of the palmettos near the end of the train. The soldiers shot him as he tried to hop across the tracks.

They lifted him into the last car and brought the members of his tribe to see him. Grey Beard said that he had wanted to die ever since he'd been chained and taken from home. He gave his old friend and war chief, Minimic, a message for his wife and daughter, and soon died.

On the road to Florida

When they arrived at Jacksonville, Florida, the sadly bedraggled Indian prisoners were moved from the railroad cars to a steamboat which would take them up the St. John's River. The guards watched as the Indians were led down the gangplank, aboard the boat.

Transfer from cars to steamboat at Jacksonville, May 21, 1875

On the steamboat the prisoners traveled upriver to the town of Tocoi. There they boarded the St. John's Railway on the last part of their journey to St. Augustine. That distance was the train's entire route— only fifteen miles.

St. John's Railway

The prisoners were brought from the train station to Fort Marion in horsedrawn carts over a covered bridge which still exists in St. Augustine. They were suffering from lingering illnesses and were doubly weak from confinement and lack of exercise. Though they hated being trapped, hated their leg irons, they were subdued and docile. They were homesick for their families and for the land they knew.

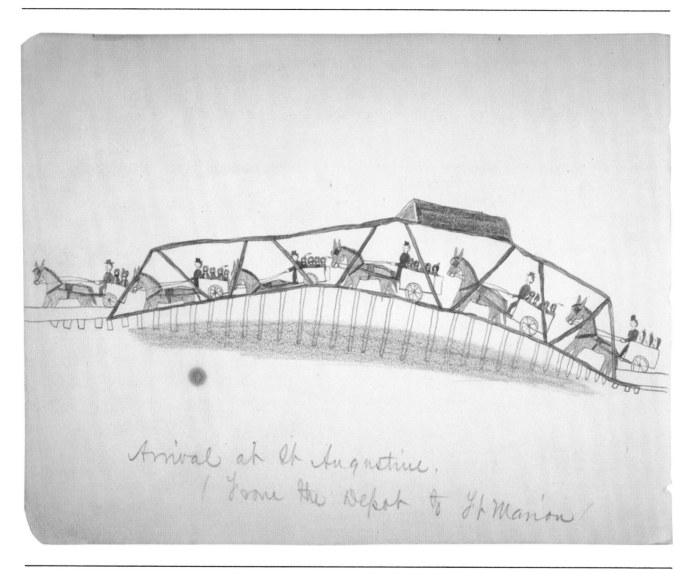

Arrival at St. Augustine (from the depot to Fort Marion)

Lieutenant Pratt, who was still in charge of the Indians at the fort, had their chains removed. And after a while, they understood that they weren't going to be killed.

A few days after the prisoners arrived at Fort Marion, Lieutenant Pratt gave them drawing books and colored pencils. Bear's Heart and many of the younger Indians began to make pages and pages of drawings. Mostly they drew pictures of life on the plains.

Curious visitors came to the fort to see the prisoners. They wanted to shake the Indians' hands and asked to have their drawings to take home as souvenirs.

Lieutenant Pratt was hoping to teach the prisoners the white man's ways and to help them find a place in the white man's world. He was glad to see them busy. And he knew that pocket money would be useful to them, so he got sea beans for them to shine. Sea beans are pale gray seeds with hard shells which the waves cast up on Florida beaches.

Pratt paid the Indians for the polished beans they brought him, which could be made into jewelry or sold as souvenirs. After a while, the prisoners also began to make small bows and arrows which they sold to the visitors. In this way, they occasionally managed to send small gifts of money back to their families.

Troops at St. Augustine

Fort Marion, a massive fortress built of white coquina rock, commanded the entrance to the harbor of St. Augustine. The Spanish had built it two hundred years before to protect their treasure ships from pirates who were based across the channel. Across the harbor was the sandy north beach, and in the middle was Anastasia Island, covered with small trees and underbrush. On the island were two lighthouses. The little one was an old Spanish lighthouse, but the big striped one was new. It had been built in 1874, the year before Bear's Heart and the other prisoners arrived.

The prisoners lived in Fort Marion for the next three years. At first, they were kept in the central court, with their only view up to the sky. They slept in huge, damp, vaulted rooms, on stone floors which had been planked over to make them more sanitary.

Entrance to harbor, St. Augustine

The Indian prisoners lived like soldiers at the fort. Their traditional clothing was taken away and they were given army outfits to wear—the off-duty uniform of an artilleryman with blue pants, a dark jacket, and a fatigue cap—though at first some of the prisoners cut off the tops of the trousers to make leggings. They started the day with setting-up exercises, performed drills, and were subject to a strict military inspection, but of course they were not allowed to have weapons.

The old stone rooms off the courtyard were miserably damp and unhealthy. In the first few months, the Indians had little resistance to diseases in the hot, humid Florida climate. Many of them had become sick, and some died.

After a while, the prisoners moved into a large, one-room barracks which they built themselves, high on the platform behind the stone parapet of the fort. In the barracks there were rows of rough board cots with mattresses stuffed with grass on either side of a wide aisle. In the center, large stoves heated the place in chilly weather.

Visitors who came to look at the prisoners saw them sitting there in the afternoons, making drawings and polishing sea beans. Trading and talking with them, the Indians began to learn English.

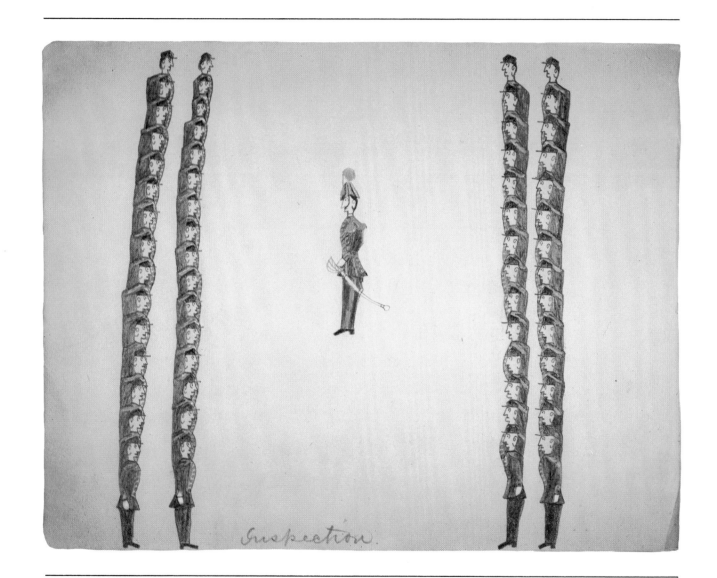

Inspection

Sometimes Lieutenant Pratt hired Mr. Pacetti, who owned a large sloop, to take the Indians out for the day to the fishing place on the north beach across from Anastasia Island. They baited a heavy shark line with eight or ten pounds of meat or fish and tied it onto a strong post in the sand. Then Mr. Pacetti rowed out, trailing the line. When he got into deep water, he dropped the baited hook. This was a favorite spot for sharks swimming in and out of the harbor.

When a shark took the bait, the Indians hauled on the rope in a real tug-of-war to pull it in, planting their feet wide apart for leverage and balance. Sometimes, when they were pulling hardest, the shark would suddenly turn and swim fast in to shore, and all the Indians would fall down. By the time they got up, it would be swimming hard away.

When the shark was worn out, it was dragged onto the sand and killed with an ax. The Indians called the shark "water buffalo" and used the sinew along its backbone for tying feathers onto the arrows they made to sell to visitors.

Catching a shark, July 1875

The pressure to conform to the white man's ways was subtle, but it never stopped. Christian values and the importance of work were preached to the prisoners. They even learned to sing hymns and were taken to church on Sundays.

Lieutenant Pratt believed that it was the government's duty to teach the Indians skills that would be permanently useful to them when they returned to their homes in the west. The Indians said they wanted to learn to build houses, to make boots and shoes, to do blacksmith work, and to farm. But the government was not helpful, and most jobs that Pratt could find for them in St. Augustine taught them nothing useful.

Catholic cathedral, St. Augustine

Some small jobs for the Indians did turn up in the neighborhood of St. Augustine. They picked and packed oranges for a short time when they came ripe each year. Five Indians helped clear palmetto and scrub from five acres of land so that a dentist from the north could start an orange grove. During the winter, when there were many northern tourists, one Indian helped the baggage handler on the Tocoi railroad.

At the fort, Lieutenant Pratt had a brick oven built, and one of the prisoners was taught to bake bread at the post bakery of the regular army barracks across town. Two other Indians served as cooks. Others worked at the town sawmill stacking lumber. They also dug a deep well for the town and even moved a large Sunday school building several blocks closer to the center of town.

The Indian prisoners became a familiar sight. People came to think of them more as strange celebrities than as prisoners, though some considered them dangerous savages and expected them to revolt at any moment. And the way people lived in St. Augustine became familiar to the Indians as well.

Meat market, St. Augustine

Lieutenant Pratt insisted that the Indian prisoners have their hair cut. But for a long time the Indians refused. They were proud of their hair; it was the last emblem of their identity they wore. Many also believed that if any of their hair fell into the hands of someone who wanted to hurt them, that person would gain magical power over them. So they certainly didn't want to risk the soldiers getting any.

The Indians were afraid of the army guards. They remembered the shooting of Grey Beard on the journey. And Pratt didn't trust the guards either. He would visit the fort late at night several times a week, never letting the guards know when he would appear.

After a while, Pratt managed to have the guards sent away. Instead, he organized a proud company of Indians to keep peace among themselves. They were also responsible for jobs like giving out supplies of food and clothing and keeping track of tools that were borrowed.

Eventually the Indians grew accustomed to the routine of prison life and became less mistrustful of their captors. Then they agreed to have their hair cut.

Indian guard at Fort Marion—marching on

In the hot summers, Lieutenant Pratt arranged for the Indians to go camping on the ocean side of Anastasia Island, just across the bay. They made the trip by sailboat. The hard beach on the ocean side of the island was good for foot races and other sports when the tide was out. And during the time they were camped there, the Indians discovered large numbers of sea beans which they gathered up to polish and sell on their own.

Going to Camp

Going to camp

Pratt borrowed army tents from the barracks for the Indians to sleep in on the island. Some men were detailed as guards to keep wild hogs from coming into the camp at night. Sometimes they caught flying fish, which were especially tasty, and roasted them over the fire.

Camping on Anastasia Island was a good time for the Indian prisoners. It was the closest they came to their old outdoor hunting life. But just because it must have reminded them of home and good times past, it was probably saddening too. Of all things, what they wanted most was to be back with their families.

In camp on Anastasia Island

Lieutenant Pratt felt that it was most important for the Indians to learn English if Indians and whites were ever to understand one another. And most of the young men did learn English during their years in prison. It became their common language. Before that, though many Indians of the southern plains understood Comanche, most could not understand one another's languages. Even the Cheyennes and the Arapahoes, who had been friendly for many years and had often made camp together, could not talk together.

Several ladies volunteered as teachers at the fort and were well liked and respected by the prisoners. They taught English using primers and pictures. Classes were held in the mornings from nine o'clock to noon in the huge, vaulted rooms of the fort with tiny, narrow windows high up in the wall. The rooms were built very solidly to be proof against bombs and cannonballs.

Miss Nannie Burt's class of Indian prisoners, Fort Marion

Early in the spring of 1876, when Bear's Heart had been at Fort Marion for nearly a year, Bishop Henry Whipple made a trip down to St. Augustine for his health. The bishop was a famous missionary and religious leader who had worked for many years among the Sioux in Minnesota. They gave him the name Straight Tongue because he was honest with them and defended them when there was trouble.

While Bishop Whipple was in St. Augustine, he preached to the Indians at the fort nine times. His words were translated into sign language by an interpreter as he spoke.

The bishop made a great impression on the Indians. In a letter, Lieutenant Pratt told him that they hardly ever made a book of pictures without putting him in it.

Bishop Whipple talking to prisoners

After three years in prison, the Indians were released. Most were returned to their reservations, but some wanted to go to school.

Pratt had tried to persuade several state agricultural colleges to admit the Indians, but the colleges considered them dangerous prisoners-of-war and refused. Pratt then wrote to General Samuel Armstrong, founder of Hampton Institute, a school for blacks in Virginia. With Pratt's assurances of their excellence and good behavior, Bear's Heart and sixteen other Cheyennes and Kiowas were admitted to Hampton. Pratt had already found people who were willing to pay for their schooling.

At Hampton, Bear's Heart learned carpentry as well as academic subjects and farming. In March of 1879, along with ten other Indians, he was baptized a Christian in the chapel of the Institute.

That fall, Pratt started an Indian school in a deserted barracks in Carlisle, Pennsylvania. But although eleven of his Indian friends went there, Bear's Heart stayed at Hampton to help make things easier for forty Sioux children who had just arrived.

Episcopal church, St. Augustine

After three years at Hampton, Bear's Heart fell sick with tuberculosis, and it was decided to send him home to Oklahoma. He spent weeks getting ready, and in April of 1881 he started home with a trunk full of gifts for his mother and friends, his chest of carpenter's tools, and a Bible.

He rode the train to Caldwell, Kansas, and went by wagon the rest of the way. After a few days of visiting, he applied at the Indian agent's office for a job. He went to work in the carpentry shop, but there was not much for him to do. A few months later he was driving a covered wagon, taking passengers to and from the train at Caldwell.

Bear's Heart always tried to make the best of things, but life on the reservation was very hard and discouraging. The pay he got for the work he did was very low. There was never enough food. The government had decided that Indians should be farmers, but the land allotted to them was not particularly suited to farming. The leaders of the tribe were not interested in the ideas Bear's Heart had brought from back East. The Indians' experiences had not given them a good opinion of white men or their ways.

In September, Bear's Heart overworked himself while helping to unload a wagon train. He was exhausted and became very sick. In January, 1882, he died. He was buried alongside the old chief, Minimic, in the agency cemetery. He was about thirty years old.

Cheyennes among the buffalo

AFTERWORD:

THE AMERICA OF BEAR'S HEART

Jamake Highwater

There are two Americas—the ancient land which existed for the ancestors of Bear's Heart for tens of thousands of years and the new America which is written about in history books. The tales of the two Americas are rarely compatible. It is for this reason that Bear's Heart's drawings are precious, providing a glimpse into the ancient land. With the exception of the histories drawn by Indians and the rare autobiographies written in English by Indians we know almost nothing about the lives and times of Native Americans before the coming of white men and their history books. So Bear's Heart's story is precious as history.

It is also important as an art form. His pictures helped to bring about the renaissance of American Indian painting, for Bear's Heart was one of the earliest "artists" who carried Indian painting into the twentieth century. He helped to invent the word "art" for his people, who had always produced it but had never named it and had never taken individual credit for creating it. Yet among the Indians, particularly of the Plains, there was hardly a person who was not a painter. The women created elaborate geometric designs while the men worked in groups to paint their shields, tepee linings, buffalo robes, and pictographic historical accounts with icons and images of their personal and tribal achievements.

As these hunters and warriors were subjugated and imprisoned far from their homes, they expressed their forlorn state and loneliness in drawings which had always been their medium of expression and of chronicling events. As you have seen, Bear's Heart was among these talented prisoners who used the white man's crayons, pencils, and inks for the first time. With amazing self-taught skills they filled army commissary books, traders' ledgers, and lengths of muslin with their traditional pictographic images, creating pictures of the undying Indian world which persisted within them. These unique creations have become known as Ledger Art, and from them has come an important influence on all the subsequent development of paintings by American Indians.

The drawings of Bear's Heart are more than art. Everywhere in his pictures is the insidious influence of his white captors and educators. It was the conviction of most white people and the official policy of the United States that Indians were not to be taught anything about their own culture—arts, languages, or religion—but were to be assimilated into white society as quickly as possible. This rule of "assimilation or annihilation" guided all Indian education until 1934, and Bear's Heart could not avoid its impact. Like many Indians prior to the present day, Bear's Heart was too trusting and too amazed by the white man's power to see what was being done to him. Therefore no rage or resentment is found in his bright, enchanted pictures, in much the way that there is no torment in the drawings of the children of Terezin concentration camp. The innocent cannot believe in the ugliness of our world and that is perhaps what makes them so vulnerable and so unbearably tragic.

Bear's Heart stayed on among the white men he admired. In May of 1880, in a little school auditorium in Virginia, he addressed in his faltering English a capacity audience of officials and students who saw in the young Cheyenne unmistakable proof that "savages" could be civilized and turned into useful human beings. "Two years I stay at St. Augustine," Bear's Heart told his audience, "then come Hampton. At Hampton I go to school and I work. When I finish my school here, I go home to teach my people to work also, I want my mother and sisters to work house, and I and brother to work farm. When they put chains on me to take me from my home, I felt sorry, but I glad now, for I good boy now."

Bear's Heart returned to his people with his short hair, his white man's clothes, and his Bible. He was a misfit though he believed he had come back to his tribe as something better than he had been when he was taken away. But his people did not agree. Bear's Heart also believed that he had discovered a vast new reality among the whites, but from the vantage of our century it seems that what he found was the grand illusion of progress which darkens our skies and muddies our rivers and sends many people in search of the values which were systematically destroyed at Indian schools. The pictures of Bear's Heart are a touching depiction of what we have lost and what Indians today are rediscovering in this ancient land newly named America.

Burton Supree is a native of New York City and a graduate of City College of New York. He is an editor for the *Village Voice,* where he writes articles on events of interest to children and on dance. Mr. Supree has also worked as a freight dispatcher, a teacher, an actor, and a choreographer-dancer, and has conducted numerous theater workshops for both children and adults. He is the co-author with Remy Charlip of two award-winning books for children, including *Harlequin and the Gift of Many Colors.*

Jamake Highwater, of Blackfeet/Cherokee parentage, is the author of many newspaper and magazine articles and several books, including Fodor's *Indian America* and *Song from the Earth: American Indian Painting.*